LOCKHEED'S CONSTELLATION

Steve Pace

Motorbooks International
Publishers & Wholesalers

Dedication

In memory of Edmund T. "Eddie" Allen, 1896–1943.

First published in 1998 by Motorbooks International Publishers & Wholesalers, 729 Prospect Avenue, PO Box 1, Osceola, WI 54020-0001 USA

Library of Congress Cataloging-in-Publication Data Available

Pace, Steve.
    Lockheed's Constellation / Steve Pace.
        p. cm. -- (Enthusiast color series)
    Includes index.
    ISBN 0-7603-0303-7 (pbk.)
    1. Constellation (Transport planes)--History. 2. Constellation (Transport planes)--Pictorial works. I. Title. II. Series.
    TL686.L6P33 1998
    629.133'340423--dc21   97-45037

On the front cover: The premier L-1049G Super G during its first flight, on 7 December 1954. A total of 16 airlines procured 101 Super Gs, and the Hughes Tool Company bought one. TWA, with 28 of them, was its biggest user. *Lockheed Martin Corporation*

On the frontispiece: The one-of-a-kind WV-2E (EC-121L, after 18 September 1962) on a manufacturer's flight test, shadowed by a T-28 Trojan chase plane. The airplane, whose giant rotodome housed an APS-82 radar unit, was created from the first WV-2 (Bu. No. 126512). *Lockheed Martin via Jeff Ethell*

On the title page: Mike Machat's dramatic illustration shows a TWA L-1049 Super G Constellation—the United States (later Star of Windsor), inbound from Kansas City and St. Louis, as it glides slowly over the New York City skyline. The setting is Christmas Eve, 24 December 1956, and the picture is entitled Home for the Holidays. *Machat Illustration*

On the back cover: A great view of the C-121A (48-609) MATS Constellation. This aircraft logged more than 16,000 hours before it was retired in 1968. *Bob Shane*

Edited by Mike Haenggi
Designed by Katie L. Sonmor

Printed in Hong Kong through World Print, Ltd.

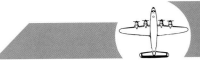

Contents

ACKNOWLEDGMENTS

This documented reference work on the Lockheed Constellation, Super Constellation, and Starliner series of aircraft could not have been produced without the generous assistance of the following individuals: Steve Ginter, Naval Fighters; Mike Machat, Machat Illustration; Denny Lombard, Lockheed Martin Skunk Works; Cheryl Gumm, AFFTC/HO; Jeff Ethell; Kirsten Oftedahl, Pima Air & Space Museum; John Accardo; John Wegg, *Airlines* Magazine; Ron Davies, National Air & Space Museum; Bud Cole, Save-A-Connie, Inc.; Dave Menard; Jane Bomar Miller; Steve Kinder; Ray Wagner, San Diego Aerospace Museum; Dennis Wrynn; Vern Raburn and Dottie Hall, Constellation Group, Inc.; Mike Lombardi, Boeing Airplane Co.; Anita DeVarney White; Scott Markham, Graphic Scenes; Don Morgan; and the publishing staff at Motorbooks International.
Steve Pace

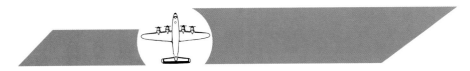

FOREWORD

I was a young child the first time I saw a Connie. My parents often took me to the airport to see my dad off on his business trips. I'd already developed a fascination with airplanes, and to my eye, the Constellation was the most beautiful one in the sky.

The early years of aviation fascinated me, and by the mid-1980s, I had bought a few vintage airplanes, including a Lockheed Lodestar. I bought the Lodestar because I'd become very interested in the historical significance of piston-engine airliners. During this period, an explosion in the interest and prices of warbirds occurred—perhaps surrounding the coming fiftieth anniversary of World War II. It seemed to me that the world would soon turn its attention to piston engine airliners, since they represented the next great leap in aviation after the war.

I bought our Connie, Serial Number 2601, in 1987. It was parked at Ryan Field in Tucson, Arizona, and was owned by actor John Travolta. Number 2601 was a military version of the Connie, known as a C-121A. Built in 1948, it was the first C-121 Constellation delivered to the newly formed U.S. Air Force (USAF). Serving initially in support of the Berlin Airlift, 2601 joined with her sister Connies in the Air Force's VIP squadron, based at National Airport in Washington, D.C. After retiring from the military in 1968, she was stored in Tucson until purchased in 1972 by a civilian operator. She was then used as a spray plane, first spraying the deserts of New Mexico for fire ants, and then the forests of Canada for budworms. This job continued until 1984, when John Travolta bought her.

Restoration work started on Number 2601 in August 1991. At that time, the plane reeked of insecticide, owls were nesting in the tail, and virtually everything in the airplane needed to be overhauled. When we stripped the paint off the aircraft, we discovered traces of the original Military Air Transport Service (MATS) markings, and decided then that she would fly as the MATS Connie, with military markings. We flew her for the first time in late 1991, but had numerous problems. During the winter of 1991–92, we focused on the engines and major systems and made the needed repairs. In the summer of 1992, the MATS Connie made her public debut at Oshkosh.

Owning and operating a plane like the Connie has been simultaneously the joy and sorrow of my life. Preserving such a significant piece of aviation history is truly both a privilege and a burden. When I sit in the left seat and watch the sunset reflect off of the 15-foot props as the sun sinks beneath the horizon, and darkness reveals the glowing exhaust flames flowing back over the nacelles, I can't help but feel the presence of the airline and military captains who explored the world with the Connie. When I see the faces of guys and gals who used to fly Connies come on board flush with memories, or just watch a modern airline pilot who has never flown a propliner fly her for the first time, the joy is immense. But when an engine fails, or a major repair is needed, or the skill to repair something is missing, the disappointment and frustration set in.

The restoration of 2601 will never really be done. Both the size of the task and the ongoing maintenance required by an operating aircraft dictate that we will always be working on and improving her. But every time I see her fly over, or whenever someone stops and thanks me for keeping her in the air, I am reminded that it's all worth it.

Vern Raburn

Pima Air & Space Museum's beautifully restored *Star of Switzerland* of TWA as it appeared in July 1996. Formerly a C-69 delivered to the USAAF on 28 July 1945 (s/n 42-94549), it now carries US registration number N90831. It took more than 7,000 hours to complete its restoration. *Kirsten Oftedahl*

INTRODUCTION

Designed in the late 1930s, the four-engine Constellation was produced in limited numbers during World War II to serve as the U.S. Army Air Force's (USAAF) C-69 transport airplane. The first version of the Connie, the Model L-49, was purchased originally by Transcontinental and Western Air and made its first flight on 9 January 1943. The aircraft, quickly drafted by the Army Air Force (AAF), had a 50-mile per hour advantage in cruise speed over any rival transport aircraft, and it was the only one in production with cabin pressurization. Pressurized cabins enabled crew and passengers to fly in air-conditioned comfort at speeds approaching 300 miles per hour at 20,000 feet, above 90 percent of troublesome weather. With its triple vertical surfaces and dolphin-like fuselage, the Connie was one of the best-looking transports ever built. Today, as a matter of fact, more than 50 years after its first appearance, it can still turn heads.

The twin-wheel main landing gears retracted forward into the inboard engine nacelles to facilitate a "free-fall" emergency gear-extension capability, and the flight controls were hydraulically powered with manual reversion—the first application of this luxury in a production transport.

The Constellation's two-spar wing incorporated integral fuel tanks and Lockheed-Fowler flaps. Typically, 50 passengers were accommodated in double seats on either side of the center aisle. Originally powered by four 18-cylinder 2,200-horsepower Wright R-3350-35 Double Cyclone engines spinning three-bladed propellers, the first L-49 had a maximum speed of 329 miles per hour at 19,800 feet, a service ceiling of 25,000 feet, and a range varying between 2,300 and 3,700 miles, depending on payload.

The first commercial version of the Connie made its initial flight on 25 August 1945, immediately after the war. At the time its principal competitors were the Boeing B-377 and the Douglas DC-4. Truly a pacesetter for its time, the Connie flew much faster, farther, and higher than its rivals.

By mid-1947, 73 model L-49s had been delivered to such major airlines as TWA, PAA, AOA, BOAC, Air France, KLM, and LAV—most of them before the first delivery of the pressurized Douglas DC-6. From this time on—from the late 1940s through the 1950s—the medium- and long-haul routes worldwide were dominated by derivatives of the Constellation and the Douglas DC-6 and DC-7 series of aircraft. Progressively more advanced versions of both series of airliners were to develop over these years, parallel to each other and in direct competition, until they were superseded by the first generation of turbojet-powered transports.

CHAPTER 1

CONSTELLATION RISING

Designed in the late 1930s, the four-engine and triple-tailed Lockheed Constellation was produced in limited numbers during World War II to serve the USAAF as a combination cargo and troop transport airplane designated C-69. The first version of the Connie (as it was nicknamed)—Lockheed model L-049-46-10, was originally procured by Transcontinental and Western Air (later Trans World Airlines or TWA) in early 1940 with a nine-plane order that was quickly upped to 40. Pan American World Airways (PAA) likewise ordered 40 L-049s, and four more were ordered by Eastern Air Lines. Thus with an 84-aircraft backlog by mid-1940, the Lockheed Aircraft Corporation in Burbank, California, happily opted to proceed with the construction of its new L-049 (or L-49) airliners. There was a new horizon in the stars for Lockheed, and its Constellation was rising above it.

Developmental Highlights

Following TWA's original order for nine L-49s in early 1940, aluminum alloy metals were fabricated, joined, and riveted together. With this, the first Constellation (civil registration number [crn] NX25600) was completed and rolled out on 23 November 1942. At this time, of course, World War II was raging. Peace was still a long way off, and as far as the U.S. airlines were concerned, the so-called "Happy Days" would have to wait. Worse, because of the war, the USAAF was

---

After U.S. Army Air Forces evaluations that ended in mid-1944, Lockheed took charge of the first Connie for its ongoing modifications and tests on the type. Shown here after it was stripped of its military camouflage identity, "Ole 1961" appears as it did prior to its initial paint job in late 1942. With a maximum takeoff weight of 86,250 pounds, this airplane was capable of 339 miles per hour with a service ceiling of 25,300 feet. *Lockheed Martin Corporation*

This is an excellent in-flight view of the eighth C-69-1-LO built (msn 4-10317), the ninth Connie produced. After the war, most C-69s were converted by the airlines for use as originally intended. It was not until the appearance of the L-749s or C-121s that the military again used them. *Lockheed Martin Corporation*

confiscating worthy passenger-carrying airliners for military duties. It was no different for Lockheed's brand-new and highly advanced Connie. Reluctantly drafted into service then, the L-49-cum-C-69s were forced to serve their nation before they could attend their paying passengers.

Having been called up by the army, instead of sporting the vibrant color schemes of the U.S. airlines, the Connie would at first wear the colors and markings of the USAAF. Wearing the official Lockheed logo on its outside vertical tail surfaces and on either side of its nose, and dressed out in olive drab green and gray camouflage war paint of the era, Connie number one was issued USAAF serial number (sn) 43-10309; Lockheed production serial number (psn) 1961. But before the Connie could

enter the war under combat conditions, it had to be proved airworthy.

There were at this time many unknowns about such a plane. In fact, because of its overall size, weight, and projected performance characteristics, it was more like a bombardment airplane than either a passenger airliner or transport. And, believe it or not, one version—Lockheed model L-51—was to be the never-built XB-30, a four-engine bomber, which lost out to the Boeing B-29 Superfortress and the Consolidated–Vultee B-32 Dominator types. Yet for those who were closely involved in the L-49/C-69 program, confidence was high. Still, beginning January 1943, Connie number one had to undergo a lengthy and challenging series of flight-test activities. These began at Burbank, continued at Muroc

Photographed from a B-25 chase plane on its initial flight, this is the first Connie to be delivered to TWA after the war. TWA took delivery of it on 15 November 1945; it was first flown on 25 August 1945. *Lockheed Martin Corporation*

Army Air Field (now Edwards Air Force Base) near Lancaster, California, and were finalized at Vandalia Field near Wright Army Air Field (now Wright-Patterson Air Force Base), Dayton, Ohio.

Flight-test Activities

When the time came for Connie number one to make its first flight, there were no experienced four-engine test pilots at Lockheed. Up the Pacific Coast in Seattle, Washington, Edmund T. "Eddie" Allen was working at the Boeing Airplane Company on its XB-29 Superfortress flight-test program. As he was a freelance test pilot with the experience required on multiengine types and with the respect of his peers, Lockheed hired him to flight-test its new Connie. He was a natural choice, since the XB-29s were pow-

ered by the same type of engine. He had made the first flight on the first of three XB-29s earlier, on 21 September 1942, and with more than three months' flying experience with this powerplant, America's most distinguished test pilot was to prove the worth of "OLE 1961," as it would later be dubbed, due to its manufacturer's psn and its long-term activities with Lockheed.

It was 9 January 1943 and time to fly. Copiloted by Lockheed single- and twin-engine chief engineering test pilot Milo Burcham, accompanied by Lockheed engineers Clarence L. "Kelly" Johnson, Dick Stanton, and Rudy Thoren, L-49 number one was prepared for flight and fired up.

Following their lengthy preflight activities and check-offs, Allen and Burcham taxied the plane from

This beautiful Confederate Air Force-owned EC-121T (ex EC-121D, ex RC-121D, USAF sn 53-548) was photographed at Camarillo Airport, just east of Ventura, California, in March 1996. It last served with the 552nd Airborne Early Warning and Control Wing (AEWCW) based at McClellan AFB near Sacramento, California. *Steve Kinder*

flight line to runway at Lockheed Air Terminal (now Burbank Airport) and stopped. After takeoff power on each of the 2,200-horsepower 18-cylinder Wright R-3350-35 engines was reached, Allen released the brakes and the first of 856 Connies, Super Connies, and Starliners began to roll. After a roll of about 5,200 feet, the airplane reached rotation speed and Allen pulled the yoke toward him. Then gracefully, Connie number one headed upward and into the winter skies above southern California.

After some 3 1/2 years of clever design and development, the airplane that was to become known as "Queen of the Skies" had taken flight. The

USAAF, TWA, PAA, and Eastern officials were in attendance and watching with great pride.

The plane flew very well indeed, and after some 50 minutes in the air with its landing gear intentionally extended throughout the flight, Allen and Burcham landed at Muroc about 100 miles northeast of Los Angeles in the Mojave Desert. And as had been planned, another five flights were flown from Muroc that same day.

After the six flights, Allen reported, "She's every bit as responsive and powerful as the '29 [XB-29] and very likely somewhat slipperier in the air. Lockheed's got a very good airplane here." Burcham, who got to sit in the left-hand seat on flights number three and five to gain experience agreed, and said, "She's a dream. I can't wait to take her up again."

Allen returned to Seattle. Unfortunately on 19 February 1943—just 41 days after he had first flown

LEFT: Flying eastward over Arizona's Grand Canyon, this is the premier TWA L-1049 Super Connie. It is shown during its delivery flight, 6 August 1952. With the advent of the L-1049, speed, range, and the number of passengers increased. *Lockheed Martin Corporation*

The USAF was first to order Super Connies, but very soon after, the USN joined ranks. Sporting silver propeller spinners, this factory-fresh WV-2 (later WV-2E then EC-121L) is shown during a Lockheed test hop. An APS-45 height-finding radar system is in the upper radome, and an APS-20B sea-search radar system is housed in the lower one. *Lockheed Martin Corporation via Jeff Ethell*

the number one Connie, he and ten others perished in the crash of XB-29 number two during a test hop out of Boeing Field.

Beginning on 26 June 1944 and ending 7 July 1944, after Lockheed had thoroughly evaluated its new plane, USAAF Lieutenant Colonel D. J. Ritland flight-tested the airplane at Burbank nine times for a total of 41 flying hours (averaging 4.5 hours per flight). Determining it had good performance and handling characteristics for all loadings from 67,000 to 90,000 pounds, and with Ritland's recommendation, it was officially accepted by the USAAF on 24 July 1944.

Between the first flight of the first Connie on 9 January 1943 and when Ritland began his evaluations on 26 June 1944, Lockheed had run a lengthy series of weight loading, center of gravity, and balance tests out of Burbank. These and numerous

This is the EC-121T (53-554, ex RC-121D) on display at the Pima Air & Space Museum, Tucson, Arizona. Named *Warning Star*, it was acquired by the PASM on 3 March 1988, and is shown as it appeared some eight years later, on 22 March 1996. *Steve Kinder*

This EC-121S, stored at Camarillo, California, was flown by the 193rd Tactical Electronic Warfare Group, which was a part of the Pennsylvania Air National Guard based at Olmstead ANG Base, Pennsylvania, in the mid-1970s. This one does not have the humps and bumps common to electronic warfare aircraft; it carries msn 54-177 and began life as a C-121C. *Mark Morgan via Steve Ginter*

other evaluations had to be completed before all-out production was authorized.

In the meantime, the USAAF waited for Connie number two to be completed and made available to its Air Transport Command (ATC) for its evaluations. In a letter dated 20 June 1944 to the commander of the ATC from the assistant chief of air staff for materiel, maintenance, and distribution, Major General Oliver P. Echols, it was stated that when number two became available, the initial flight tests would be over six to seven weeks and would cover long-range performance data, maximum-range data, optimum power data, and three- and two-engine data.

The number two Connie was completed in June 1944, and after its first flight, it was ferried to Vandalia Field in Ohio.

Two months earlier, on 17 April 1944, the number one Connie was to be ferried to Wright AAF in

Ohio for a high-ranking look-see by the USAAF's ATC. To fully exploit an opportunity for future business and freely advertise its unique performance, TWA president Jack Frye and major TWA stockholder Howard R. Hughes, Jr., received permission to attempt a new transcontinental speed record during the long-way-around flight. At TWA's expense, the airplane was decked out in the colors of TWA; it had earlier been stripped of its camouflage warpaint.

With Hughes and Frye at the controls, Connie number one flew at 17,000 feet from Los Angeles to Washington, D.C., in an elapsed time of six hours, 57 minutes, and 51 seconds. A new record had been established and TWA's future Connie passengers had been fully enticed. Record in hand, Hughes and Frye continued on to Vandalia Field, where the airplane was thoroughly eyeballed before its return to Burbank on 3 May 1944.

This is the first of 10 RC-121C aircraft (51-3836) as it appeared in November 1961. It was later reclassified to trainer status and was redesignated TC-121C, then EC-121C after 1962. *W. M. Jefferies via Dave Menard*

RIGHT: On 29 September 1962, the fourth C-121A (now as a VC-121A; msn 48-612) was photographed after receiving day-glo tail markings. It had served earlier as a C-121A in the Atlantic Division of the USAF MATS. It later received Civil Register No. N9465; final disposition unknown. *W. M. Jefferies via Dave Menard*

It should be noted that the first L-49/C-69 and at least the first nine production examples came equipped with single-speed superchargers on their engines. As soon as the Wright Company perfected its two-speed blowers, later Connies had them. For a time, if not perfected, the USAAF had opted for radial 2,000-horsepower Pratt & Whitney R-2800 Double Wasp engines for its C-69s. To test the application, C-69 number one (temporarily redesignated XC-69E) received the R-2800 engines for tests. But Wright's two-speed superchargers proved adequate, and all C-69s retained their Wright R-3350 engines.

Howard Hughes accomplished many things in his lifetime, and in fact, the design of aircraft

This is the only VC-121E (msn 53-7885) to ever appear. While on the Lockheed assembly line as a USN R7V-1 (Bu. No. 131650), it was modified to serve as a special USAF VIP transport. It became *Columbine III*, President Eisenhower's third Connie, and served as *Air Force One* until President Kennedy began using his Boeing VC-137C jetliner in October 1962. The one-of-a-kind VC-121E was later assigned to the 89th Military Airlift Group at Andrews Air Force Base, Maryland, as a *plain* VIP transport. It has been at the USAF Museum, Dayton, Ohio, since 1980. *Major D. Mikler via Dave Menard*

was one of his many successes. But contrary to many beliefs, he *did not* design the Lockheed Constellation. In truth, Hughes and Frye had only delivered to Lockheed their specific requirements for such an airliner. More to the point, if Hughes had designed it, his company, Hughes Aircraft, would have built it.

Initially started as the model L-44 Excalibur program in early 1939, the project grew to become model L-49 Excalibur A by mid-1939. And after

This is the first of nine C-121A aircraft (msn 48-609) in the later polished aluminum and white color scheme, after its modification to VC-121A standard. This particular airplane would later play a large role in Vern Raburn's life, as it is the airplane he owns and operates today—the MATS Connie, discussed elsewhere. *Ron Picciani via Steve Ginter*

TWA put money down, the L-49 program metamorphosed into the Constellation project. Soon after, Lockheed's Don Palmer was assigned to the program as project engineer.

Hall Hibbard and Kelly Johnson had outlined to Palmer a unique concept for a new and improved air-

liner. He was to later say: "Their approach to TWA's requirements was, at the very least, brilliant. For example, to deal with the ever-enlarging vertical tail areas required for additional stability on ever-growing aircraft sizes, Johnson, already a firm believer in two-tailed aircraft, came up with the novel tri-tailed

THE DEVELOPMENT OF THE LOCKHEED CONSTELLATION

BY KELLY JOHNSON

On 30 November 1944, some 22 months after the first Connie appeared in the skies over southern California, Lockheed chief research engineer Kelly Johnson presented a paper to the Los Angeles section of the Institute of Aeronautical Sciences. He discussed thoroughly the engineering testing and research on the basic design problems of a large transport airplane. Some highlights of his paper—only to make clear some misleading information found in other references on the Connie—are as follows:

"The initial design studies for this airplane were first undertaken in June 1939. The Lockheed L-49 Constellation, known also by the USAAF designation of C-69, was conceived as a long-range, high-speed, high-altitude transport, for which low operating cost was a basic requirement. The flight characteristics desired were to be a substantial improvement over those of existing aircraft, with maximum controllability available for all emergency, as well as normal, flight conditions.

"Designed from the outset as a four-engine transport plane, the first problem encountered concerned the size of the engine to be used. It was soon apparent that the best airplane for the task would be one equipped with very large engines, operating at a low percentage of their rated power, with the minimum possible degree of supercharging. Thus, we selected the 2,200-horsepower, 18-cylinder, air-cooled Wright R-3350-35 Double Cyclone engine, with a 3,350-cubic inch displacement.

"The question is frequently asked why the fuselage shape of the Constellation is so unusual. The explanation is very simple. In order to reduce the length of the nose landing gear, which was already very long due to the large diameter of the three-bladed propellers, the mean camber line of the fuselage was lowered for the forward section of the fuselage. To reduce the drag at the maximum lift-to-drag ratio of the plane, a slight downward curvature was also employed aft of the wing. This gave the fuselage a basic shape corresponding roughly to the mean flow line over the wing at cruising speed; result, decreased drag.

"The first flight of the Constellation took place on 9 January 1943. Previous to that date, extensive preparations had been made for complete flight testing on all components of the airplane. Having completed the preflight tests, the airplane was taken off and flown on six different flights the first day. After a 50-minute first flight, the airplane was landed at Muroc Army Air Field [now Edwards Air Force Base], and there, five more flights were made. No difficulty was experienced on these flights, so the formal flight-test program was undertaken.

"On 17 April 1944, the first Constellation was flown at high altitude from Los Angeles to Washington, D.C., in an elapsed time of six-hours, 57 minutes, and 51 seconds. The Constellation is expected to repeat this type of performance in the future during its service with the U.S. Air Forces and later with the world's airlines."

The legendary Kelly Johnson, founder of the famed Skunk Works, is credited with the design of some forty Lockheed aircraft—including the Constellation. After numerous years of duty to Lockheed and his country, at the age of 80, he passed away on 21 December 1990.

This EC-121T (msn 54-2307), photographed on 25 August 1978, is unique because it was the very last one to be on station in the United Kingdom. It first served with the 79th Airborne Early Warning Squadron, and later with the USAF Reserves at Homestead AFB, Florida. *G. W. Pennick via Dave Menard*

arrangement to enhance flying qualities and accommodate maintenance in existing hangers used by the airlines." He added, "Hibbard, sometimes more magical than anything else, raked the nose downward so that the nose landing gear would not only be shorter in length but much stronger and stable." Palmer concluded, "Of course there were many other innovations on the Connie by these two engineering wizards. But these limited examples exemplify from where I speak."

Therefore when the premier L-49 Constellation appeared in late 1942, she was not only pleasing to look at, she was well-engineered and easily ahead of her time, with her graceful dolphin-like shape featuring three tails. Large as she was, she seemed to be flying, but was not moving. It would be another two years before she would go into service with the military, another four years for the airlines. But the wait, as would later be proved, turned out to be worthwhile.

"You're in the Army Now, You're Not Behind a Plow"

Since the United States had entered the war one year earlier on, 8 December 1941, new airline-ordered Connies with the military designation C-69 rolled off the production line. Now playing the roll of cargo and troop transport aircraft, they began to enter service with the USAAF ATC in mid-1945. But, due to their late appearance, only 15 C-69s were actually on duty when V-J Day came at 10:30 A.M. Tokyo time on 2 September 1945. As a matter of interest, during the war, the USAAF ATC employed a total of 22,070 transport-type aircraft. And although the C-69s were excellent examples of these cargo aircraft, which included the likes of the Curtiss C-46 Commando, Douglas C-47 Skytrain, and C-54 Skymaster—in only two months of action, they did not have a great deal of time to prove their value. Nor did they ever go overseas.

This EC-121S (msn 54-159) shows the lumps and bumps associated with electronic warfare aircraft. It is shown on final approach to Olmstead ANG Base in Pennsylvania, circa 1975. *Ron Picciani via Steve Ginter*

Based at McGuire AFB, New Jersey, this C-121C (msn 54-175) belonged to the New Jersey National Guard in May 1972, when it was captured in this freeze frame. The USAF procured 33 C-121Cs, which were similar to USN R7V-1s, but powered by the USAF version of the 3,510-horsepower R-3350 engines. *Steve Miller via Dave Menard*

This is one of only five NASA-operated C-121Gs (msn 54-4076), photographed in May 1973, at Davis-Monthan AFB, Tucson, Arizona. After its retirement, it most likely was scrapped. It carried NASA register number 421; there were only 33 Gs, all former R7V-1s. *P. B. Lewis via Dave Menard*

But during those two months of limited Connie operations, U.S. soldiers fully appreciated their good fortunes being able to ride on such a fast and high-flying transport. Having made several cross-country flights during his wartime service on C-47s, First Lieutenant William T. "Bill" Robinson said: "Flying on C-47s was at the very least boring, and for the most part, unsettling. With three and sometimes four stops to take on more fuel, drop off passengers, pick up passengers, and so on, it took forever to fly coast-to-coast." He went on, "Worse,

since the C-47s couldn't get above most storms, they had to fly around them or through them. In other words, with all the buffeting and sudden drops, barf bags were a valued commodity. He concluded: "On 5 August 1945, I was lucky enough to fly home. Most guys had to ride trains. In any event, my flight was from Bolling Field in Washington, D.C., for a trip westward to March Field near Riverside, California. This time I got a seat on a plane I didn't even know existed—a C-69—and to my surprise, it flew all the way to March Field nonstop!

Filmed in September 1979, at Davis-Monthan AFB, this USN EC-121K (Bu. No. 141297) began life as a WV-2. Just before it was parked here, it had served with the USN's Research Laboratory, flying such missions as monitoring ice-flow patterns in the North Atlantic. It, and others, also kept sharp eyes on the Soviet Union's fishing fleet which, as time has proved, did not catch many fish. *Brian Baker via Dave Menard*

Moreover, it flew much higher than the two C-47s I'd flown on before. So the ride was much smoother and a lot more enjoyable."

Good as the C-69 was at war's end, there were many, many more Douglas C-54s available. So until the arrival of later versions of the Connie for military use, namely the model 749-79-36 or C-121A, first ordered in early 1948, the C-54 was the standard four-engine transport.

And beginning in the summer of 1949, the U.S. Navy started employment of Airborne Early Warn-

ing or AEW Connies with the designation of PO-1W (model 749A-79-43).

For service with its relatively new MATS formed on 1 June 1948, the USAF (from 18 September 1947 and on) placed an initial order with Lockheed for nine C-121As and a single VC-121B to be fitted out as a VIP transport, possibly to be used by then President Harry S. Truman. Powered by 2,500-horsepower Wright R-3350-75 engines, in 1950, C-121As number 2 through 10 were converted to VC-121As. The VC-121B, instead of becoming a presidential aircraft, served as a VIP transport.

Naval Air Station Patuxent River, Maryland, is the USN's flight-test and evaluation facility. This NC-121K (Bu. No. 145924) of VXN-8 was pictured there 11 June 1970. These aircraft were used for special missions—even in the Arctic. *Steve Miller via Dave Menard*

Before conversion to VC-121A standard, between 26 June 1948 and 31 October 1949, seven C-121As were used in the Berlin Airlift. This action helped supply food and other necessities to those people cut off from their normal supply chains when Russia started to put its infamous Berlin Wall between East and West Germany.

When World War II ended, since the soon-to-be USAF had standardized its fleet of C-54s, 12 of 15 C-69s on hand were immediately sold as surplus.

The L-49 Connie was at last going to be used for what it had been originally designed for, that is, to transport paying airline passengers.

Postwar Demand

So as the late 1940s arrived, the world's airlines began their demands for high-altitude, high-capacity, and high-speed airliners. The Constellation more than met their requirements, and without hesitation, the airlines ordered them in near-record droves.

This is the same NC-121K (Bu. No. 145924) two years later, named *El Coyote* while at Eglin AFB, Florida. After participating in Projects Magnet and Birdseye, *El Coyote* did earn some fame during Project Outpost Seascan. It belonged to the Atlantic Fleet and carried the JB tail code. *D. B. Colbert via Dave Menard*

Soon 82 of the 88 L-49/C-69 aircraft had gone into service with the airlines. Air France got four; seven went to American Overseas Airlines (a division of American Airlines); British Overseas Airlines Company (BOAC) received six; Capitol Airlines bought two; four went to Intercontinental US; Dutch airlines (KLM) procured six; two went to Lineas Aereas Venezolanas (LAV); Pan Am purchased 20; and TWA grabbed 31.

Suddenly, instead of now classic DC-3s filling the skies above the world, much more modern airliners had appeared. It was the Connie that led the way.

This is the sleek-looking Save-A-Connie Super G (ex L-1049H), Civil Register No. N6937C, in its natural environment somewhere near Kansas City, Missouri. This was one of three L-1049Hs that Slick Airways owned. SAC wanted to finish it in TWA markings, but insurance regulations would not allow it. *The Save-A-Connie Organization*

An RC-121D (msn 52-3425), with one engine out and flaps dumped, makes a routine landing at Otis AFB, Massachusetts, in 1957. The USAF procured 73 of this type, redesignated EC-121D in 1962, which featured WV-2 styled radomes and wingtip fuel tanks. *P. Paulsen via Dave Menard*

CHAPTER 2

CIVILIAN CONNIES

As mentioned earlier, TWA, Eastern, and Pan Am first ordered the advanced L-49 Constellations for civilian passenger transportation duties. Starting in late 1945 and early 1946, these airlines began receiving their Connies which, before entering daily service, were used to train their flight crews. In one instance, this went like this:

In a ceremony at Burbank on 14 November 1945, TWA chief pilot Capt. Robert N. "Bob" Buck took delivery of TWA's first L-49, which had made its initial flight on 25 August 1945. Buck and his crew ferried the plane (crn N86536, Lockheed sn 1979) to TWA's home base in Kansas City, Missouri, to initiate crew training. And on 6 February 1946, regular flights between Washington, D.C., New York, and Paris were inaugurated.

TWA Captain Bob Buck would go on to log more than 9,000 flying hours domestically and internationally on every civilian version of the Connie. He would later concede that the L-749A model was his favorite version, but that the "model L-1649A Starliners were the greatest long-range [piston-powered and propeller-driven] airliners ever built." He piloted them from Los Angeles to London on a regular basis, and his only squawk was the plane's "troublesome turbo-compound engines," to be discussed later. Mrs. Jane Bomar Miller, wife of TWA Captain John Miller, was a flight attendant for TWA during the 1944 to 1947 period. She initially served aboard DC-3s, then B-307s, and finally L-49s, and was part of the crew when TWA's first Connie was ferried to Kansas City. She flew in an era when "stewardesses had to look like Lana Turner," she said. "You couldn't wear glasses, your weight had to be proportional to your height, and your complexion had to

The premier L-1049G Super G during its first flight, on 7 December 1954. A total of 16 airlines procured 101 Super Gs, and the Hughes Tool Company bought one. TWA, with 28 of them, was its biggest user. *Lockheed Martin Corporation*

At one time, as the largest unscheduled operator of Connies and Super Connies, Capitol International Airways operated a 23-aircraft fleet, comprising L-749As, L-1049Es, L-1049Gs, and L-1049Hs. Their first was this L-749A (Civil Register No. N5401V), which it acquired in 1957. *Lockheed Martin Corporation*

This was the first L-1049H Super Connie (Civil Register No. N6911C) to go to the Flying Tiger line; it eventually bought 13 of this type. First flight of this type, which could be quickly converted from all-cargo to all-passenger modes, was on 20 September 1956. *Lockheed Martin Corporation*

This is an American Flyers Airline Corporation L-1049E (Civil Register No. N9639Z). Based in Fort Worth, Texas, AFA began its Connie activities in April 1960, after it had acquired four L-049s. By the end of 1968, its Connie/Super Connie fleet had been retired. *Lockheed Martin Corporation*

be spotless." She went on, "We had to memorize the names of all the passengers and address them that way. We had to wear gloves and hats, and when the passengers left the plane, we had to escort them to an airport's restaurant."

Jane married John in 1947, and since the airlines did not allow married women to fly in those days, she was forced to quit the job she loved. Her husband was promoted to captain in 1955 and retired in 1977. He recalled some of the vicious thunderstorms he was forced to fly around and through while at the controls of Connie aircraft. He said, "In those days we didn't have any radar onboard. Everything came from a tower," he said. "They'd spot the buttes (thunderheads) for us, but they'd move so quickly they'd be on top of us before we knew it."

John had met his wife on a "white-knuckles" flight into Albuquerque, New Mexico, when an "indicator light on an instrument panel said the plane's landing gear had failed to extend." His future wife said, "I peeked into the cockpit where the crew appeared to be calm, but no matter, I was secretly running the beads of my rosary through my fingers."

Miller flew in low over the tower several times, while the air traffic controllers attempted to verify

An L-1049G (PP-VDE) purchased by the Brazilian airline Empresa de Viacao Aerea Rio Grandense (VARIG). Initially, VARIG bought six L-1049Gs, and later the line acquired four L-1049Hs. In addition to the Super Connie prototype, created from the very first Connie, Lockheed built a total of 578 examples. It was by far the most successful version of the breed. *Lockheed Martin Corporation*

An artist's concept of what the L-1649 Starliner was to look like. These illustrations, in addition to much data, are presented to potential customers prior to a new type's manufacturing processes. *Lockheed Martin Corporation*

that the plane's landing gear had extended. Though the light in the cockpit said otherwise, the controllers in the tower convinced him the gear was down, and he safely landed the plane.

The flight crew's ensuing job was to coax some of the unwilling passengers back on the plane for the next leg of the flight.

The first dedicated commercial version of the L-49 Connie was powered by four 2,200-horsepower Wright 745C-18BA-1 Double Cyclone engines. Its first flight came about on 25 August 1945. At that time in

RIGHT: The premier Starliner (Civil Register No. N1649), at first to be called the Super Star Constellation, was Lockheed's response to Douglas' DC-7C—the former's major competition until the arrival of the Boeing 707, Convair 880, and Douglas DC-8 jetliners. The first Starliner demonstrated a speed of 380 miles per hour at an altitude of 18,500 feet. Ultimately, since the jet age had arrived, only 44 examples were built. Only three airlines—Air France, Lufthansa, and TWA—used them. *Lockheed Martin Corporation*

This beautiful L-1049G look-alike of the Save-A-Connie organization, based in Kansas City, Missouri, was previously an L-1049H Super Connie owned by Slick Airways. Keeping its 3,400-horsepower turbo-compound engines (150 more horsepower more than the engines on the Gs), this particular H was originally procured on 30 September 1959 as the last *undelivered* Super Connie. It still carries its original crn N6937C. *Save-A-Connie*

history, its principal competition came from Boeing's B-377 Stratocruiser and Douglas' DC-4. A proposed competitor that was never built was the Republic Rainbow, another four-engine airliner based on Republic's ill-fated R-12 photographic reconnaissance plane. (Only two XR-12s were built.) Truly a pacesetter for its time, however, the Connie flew faster, farther, and higher than any of its contemporaries.

Worldwide Success

By mid-1947, 73 civil L-49s had been delivered to such major airlines as American Overseas Airlines, or AOA; Air France; British Overseas Airways Company (BOAC); Koninklijke Luchvaart Naatschappi, pany (BOAC); Koninklijke Luchvaart Naatschappi,

or KLN; Lineas Aeropostal Venezolana (LAV); Pan American World Airways, or PAA; and Trans World Airlines (TWA). Most of these were delivered before the pressurized version of the Douglas DC-6.

In any event, from the late 1940s to the early 1960s, the medium- to long-haul worldwide air lanes were dominated by derivatives of DC-6s, DC-7s, Connies, and Super Connies.

Progressively more advanced versions of the above series of airliners developed over the years, parallel to each other and in direct competition, until, of course, they were all supplemented and ultimately replaced by the first wave of turbojet-powered passenger airliners and cargo transports.

The classic dolphin-like shape of the original L-49 Connies is illustrated in this side view of the ninth C-69 delivered to the USAAF on 28 July 1945 (msn 42-94549). Now more than 50 years old, after restoration, it shines like new at the Pima Air & Space Museum in Tucson, Arizona. *Kirsten Oftedahl*

NEXT; In August 1979, John Accardo of Shirley, New York, shot this photograph of a lonely looking L-1049H (C-FBDB, CF-BDB prior to 1975) at Stephenville, Newfoundland. The large door aft of the left wing and the small number of windows identify it as a cargo carrier. When Accardo took this photo, he inquired about it at the airport. Airport personnel told him they didn't know much, but there had been two Connies, and one was made flyable and flown out by "some guys from Texas." This 1049H was registered by the Canadian government and was most likely operated by Downair of Newfoundland, which ceased operations in late 1973. *John Accardo*

This L-749A, shot at Santa Cruz, Bolivia, in 1994, was owned by Trans Bolivian Airlines, which, for some unknown reason, never operated it. It carries Registration Number CP-797 No. 1 (4) and appears to be on permanent display at an unknown location. *Steve Kinder*

In the case of the Connie and Super Connie, a number of significant models evolved, beginning with original L-49. These evolved as follows:

Connie Versions

The L-649, powered by more powerful 2,500-horsepower Wright 749C-18BD-1 engines, made its first flight on 18 October 1946; it carried crn NX101A. Beginning in May 1947, Eastern Air Lines took delivery of 14 L-649s, and this was the first version of the Connie to be equipped with the so-called "Speedpack," a removable storage unit that carried up to 8,200 pounds, mounted ventrally.

The L-749, powered by the same engines that powered the L-649s, was the first Connie designed from the outset for overseas flights.

Super Connie Versions

The first L-1049 Super Connie, flown on 13 October 1950, was created from the original L-49 Connie by stretching its fuselage 18 feet five inches. The first production L-1049 made its maiden flight on 14 July 1951, and entered service on 7 December of that year. These were powered by 2,700-horsepower Wright 956C-18CA-1 engines.

The L-1049C, first to use the Wright 872TC-18DA-1 Turbo-Compound engine in its original form, made its first test hop on 17 February 1953. This engine, rated at 3,250 horsepower for takeoff, reduced fuel consumption by 20 percent and boosted overall performance.

The L-1049D was a convertible cargo- or passenger-carrying aircraft, powered by the same

This L-749A Super Connie, based in Tucson, Arizona, and photographed in March 1996, carries the markings of Conifair Aviation of Canada. This is one of three 749s that Conifair converted to sprayers to serve the Canadian Department of Lands and Forests. *Steve Kinder*

engines as above. It entered service in 1954 with Seaboard and Western Airlines.

The L-1049Es, of which 28 examples were delivered between May 1954 and April 1955 to eight airlines, was a clone to the L-1049C, except for its higher operating weight.

The L-1049G or Super G, first flown on 7 December 1954, was the best received version of the Super Connie. Introduced first by Northwest Airlines, the 'G' was powered by 3,400-horsepower Wright 972TC-18DA-3 Turbo-Cyclone/Turbo-Compound, and as an option, was fitted with wingtip fuel tanks for longer range. When Super G production ended, U.S. carriers had taken delivery of 42 of them (TWA bought 28, Eastern Air Lines purchased 10, and Northwest Airlines procured 4). Foreign airlines were

Derelict, this TWA L-1649A Starliner (Civil Register No. N7315C) was in shambles at Anchorage, Alaska, circa July 1993. Of the 44 examples produced, TWA owned and operated 29 of them. Some 70 miles per hour faster than its DC-7C rival, Starliners were able to fly from New York to Paris about three hours quicker than the *Seven Seas*. *Steve Kinder*

the biggest user of this type, having bought 59 examples (Air France, 14; Lufthansa, 8; KLM and VARIG, 6 each; Air-India, 5; TCA or Trans-Canada Airlines, 4; TAP or Transportes Aereas Portugueses of Portugal and Thai Airways, 3 each; Iberia, LAV, and QANTAS, 2 each; and Avianca, 1). One was bought by the Hughes Tool Company as a privately owned transport.

The L-1049H, first flown on 20 September 1956, was the last civilian version of the Super Connie. This was a passenger/cargo convertible version powered as the L-1049G.

Put into service in October 1956, 53 examples materialized before production ended. Five foreign airlines bought 13 of them (Aerovias Real, 4; PIA or Pakistan International Airlines, 2; QANTAS, 2; TAC, 2; and KLM, 3). Nine U.S. carriers bought the other 40 examples (Air Finance Corporation, 3; California Eastern, 5; Dollar Airlines, 1; Flying Tigers, 13; National Airlines, 4; Resort Airlines, 2; Seaboard and Western, 5; Slick Airways, 3; and TWA, 4. Basically, the L-1049H was a much improved version of the L-1049D, with the additional improvements enjoyed by the L-1049H.

With engine number four fired up and running, this Santo Domingo-based Aerolineas Mundo S.A. (AMSA) L-1049H Super Connie prepares for flight in March 1990. Unfortunately, it crashed the next day. AMSA also operated a C-121C (HI-515) out of Santa Domingo in the Dominican Republic. *Steve Kinder*

As if they realize it will not play anymore, a flock of birds leave a former playmate, which is for the most part derelict, at Ryan Field near Tucson, Arizona, in March 1996. It remains unclear whether this L-749 will be restored or scrapped. *Steve Kinder*

Enter the Starliner

At first called the Super Star Constellation, the model L-1649A Starliner was the essence of what the Connie/Super Connie was all about, the epitome of what Kelly Johnson had foreseen in the summer of 1939. First flown on 11 October 1956, the premier Starliner was Lockheed's answer to Douglas' DC-7C Seven Seas. And naturally, it was TWA that got the ball rolling with an order for 25 examples in 1955.

Obviously, if you look closely, the Starliner was molded from the matrix enjoyed by the L-1049G Super Connie but with an all-new wing platform with a thinner airfoil. And it came powered with Wright 988TC-18EA-2 Turbo-Cyclone compound engines, which delivered 3,400 horsepower. Moreover, since its engine placement was farther outboard, its passengers were not as overwhelmed with powerplant noise.

With the advent of the B-707, DC-8, and CV-880 jet-powered airliners in 1958–1959, however, the propliners—250 miles per hour slower—were quickly abandoned by domestic and foreign carriers. As good as the Starliner was, just 44 examples were built for only three customers. TWA got 29, Air France bought 10, Lufthansa procured 4, and Lockheed kept the prototype.

The first TWA-owned L-1649A Starliner entered service in May 1957, in what TWA called its Jetsream Fleet. On 2 October 1957, TWA started over-the-pole service between Los Angeles

This L-49, formerly operated by Edde Airlines of North Hollywood, California, was photographed at Fort Lauderdale, Florida, in March 1990. Since Edde Airlines has not operated since 1966, this airplane, when photographed, had apparently been parked for 24 years. Registered as Civil Register No. N90816, it was the 20th L-49 to go originally to TWA; it may be scrapped by now. *Steve Kinder*

This L-49, formerly a C-69-1-LO delivered in January 1946 to the 502nd USAAF Base Unit of the Air Transport Command at La Guardia International Airport in New York, now resides at Pima Air & Space Museum in TWA colors—named *Star of Switzerland*, crn N90831. *Steve Kinder*

Flying over the pole, Air France flew its first Starliner from Los Angeles to Paris, 5,800 miles nonstop in a new record time of 17 hours and 11 minutes. Not to be outdone, Lufthansa flew its first L-1649A nonstop from Burbank to Hamburg, Germany, in 17 hours and 19 minutes—total distance, 7,000 miles.

Still, the new jetliners were superior in every way to the old propliners. The Connie, Super Connie, and Starliner fleets of civilian aircraft, operated by flocks of domestic and foreign airlines, were well received and more than successful. But in the end, they were overtaken by the progress they helped to create.

In 1993, Steve Kinder photographed this impounded ex-USN R7V-1, converted to civilian L-1049 standard (crn N4247K), at Manila in the Philippines. It is not clear why it was impounded or what airline operated it. *Steve Kinder*

Its better days gone, this L-1049C at Santa Domingo in the Dominican Republic appeared to be rotting away when it was photographed in March 1990. First used as a passenger airliner, it was later reduced to the role of a sprayer. *Steve Kinder*

This civilian freighter version of the L-1049 was quite similar to USAF C-121Cs. This one, at Opa Locka, Florida, is an L-1049H (Civil Register No. N1007C) formerly operated by Trans-Canada Airlines, as it appeared in March 1990; final disposition is unknown. *Steve Kinder*

CHAPTER 3

MILITARY CONNIES

Long before the birth and the first flight of the Constellation in early 1943, Lockheed had more than proved its worth as a viable airplane manufacturer. At this time, in fact, it had already designed, developed, and produced such notable aircraft as the Hudson bomber, Lightning fighter, Lodestar transport, Ventura bomber, and Harpoon patrol bomber. Each one of these types had greatly contributed to the allied victories over Germany, Italy, Japan, and their axis friends.

While it is true that the C-69 Constellation's late entry into the war did not contribute much to its success as a warbird, the plane itself demonstrated superior performance as a dedicated military troop and cargo transport airplane. And even before the war ended, Lockheed had initiated further design studies to improve its already good airplane. In late 1947, a revised version of the original L-49/C-69 aircraft was offered to the newly established USAF and its MATS. This new version—Lockheed model L-749A-79-36—was projected as a cargo- and/or personnel-carrying transport based on the postwar model 749A being enjoyed by U.S. and foreign airlines. In February 1948, the USAF ordered nine examples designated C-121A and one other designated VC-121B. The latter version was to be used as a VIP transport (sn 48-608). In another move, two L-749A airframes were modified to meet U.S. Navy standards. These two Connies, ordered in June 1948, served as combat information center and AEW aircraft designated PO-1W (model 749A-79-43).

The first of 10 originally ordered C-121 aircraft as the VC-121B (USAF sn 48-608) was initially delivered to the 1254th Air Transport Squadron (Special Missions) at Washington National Airport, later based at Andrews AFB. Built as a VIP transport and for possible use by President Truman, it is shown here as it appeared in July 1970. Originally named *Dewdrop*, it was first used by General Hoyt Vandenberg. *Dave Menard Collection*

The beautifully restored MATS Connie at Tucson, Arizona, in March 1996. The Connie Group thrilled thousands of spectators that year, when its rare L-749A appeared at air shows and other events. It is the very first production C-121A airplane. *Steve Kinder*

The MATS Connie

In 1987 businessman and computer software entrepreneur Vern Raburn—who collects, restores, and operates many classic aircraft—bought from movie and TV actor John Travolta the first C-121A (48-609) to go into service with the USAF/MATS in 1948.

This now rare model L-749A (msn 2601), having served in the 1948 Berlin Airlift and as a VIP transport designated VC-121A, logged more than 16,000 flying hours before its retirement in 1968.

Then 19 years later in 1987, totally dedicated to the restoration of this historic airplane, Vern Raburn made his plans.

Restoration work began in August 1991, and the MATS Connie returned to the skies in June 1992 for a limited air show tour. Extensive additional restoration work was conducted throughout the winter of 1992–1993. Raburn, founder of the Constellation

Following use by NASA, the number five C-121A (msn 2605; USAF sn 48-613), formerly the *Bataan* used by General of the Army Douglas MacArthur, was restored. Now carrying its former VC-121A designation, displaying NASA Registration Number N422NA, it is shown here at McClellan AFB, near Sacramento, California, in March 1995. Previously, it had been displayed at Fort Rucker, Alabama. *Steve Ginter*

Group, Inc., dedicated to the restoration of classic aircraft, shows the Connie and offers pilots a chance to fly it. Eventually, the Connie Group plans to outfit the entire interior of its L-749A as a flying museum.

U.S. Government Connies and Super Connies

The U.S. government was a big user of the Connie and Super Connie aircraft. Used first by the U.S. Army Air Forces, second by the U.S. Air Force, third by the U.S. Navy, fourth by the U.S. Air Force National Guard, fifth by the U.S. Air Force Reserves, sixth by the U.S. Army, and lastly by the National Aeronautics and Space Administration and others, its easy to see why it was such a wide-ranging user of these airplanes.

USAAF Connies

The C-69 series, of which only 15 were used by the USAAF before war's end, came into the fold as follows: ten C-69-1-LOs, one C-69C-1-LO, and four

C-69-5-LOs. The first of the ten C-69-1-LO airplanes (the original Connie) reverted back to Lockheed. The one-off C-69C (42-94550) was used as a VIP transport, and before it was sold as surplus in 1948, it had been redesignated ZC-69C-1-LO. To serve as an engine testbed, the first C-69 Connie (43-10309) was fitted with four 2,100-horsepower Pratt & Whitney R-2800-83 engines and carried the temporary designation XC-69E-LO. The P&W R-2800 series of engines were very good indeed, but never used to power any version of the Connie.

There was, of course, the nine C-121As and single VC-121B previously discussed. These were much improved versions of the C-69 series of aircraft.

USN Super Connies

The USN, first customer to buy military Super Connies, ultimately procured 202 examples under various designations for a number of different uses. These included the PO-2W (to WV-1), the WV-2 (to

The number four C-121A (later VC-121A; msn 48-612) shows different USAF markings at Hamilton AFB in 1956 and at McCarran AFB on 21 September 1962. In the first pose, its markings are those of USAF/MATS and, in the second pose, its markings are those of a dedicated VC-121A VIP transport. *W. M. Jeffries via Dave Menard*

The restored *Columbine* first used by General of the Army Dwight Eisenhower when he was commander of Supreme Headquarters, Allied Powers in Europe (SHAPE). After Eisenhower became president, he used the second C/VC-121A (msn 48-610) and named it *Columbine II*. The first *Columbine* is shown at Pima Air & Space Museum at Tucson, Arizona, in the summer of 1996. This plane was first delivered to the 1600th Air Transport Group, Westover AFB, Maine, on 4 February 1949; it retired in June 1967. *Kirsten Oftedahl*

WV-2E, EC-121L, EC-121K), the R7V-1 (to C-121J), and the WV-3 (to WC-121N).

USAF Super Connies

The USAF, beginning with the C-121A and VC-121B, ultimately bought 190 Super Connies, and eventually acquired a number more from the USN. These included the C-121C, the C-121G, the EC-121R, the RC-121C (to EC-121D), the RC-121D (to EC-121D), the VC-121E, and two prototype YC-121Fs. The prototypes were a proposed version powered by four 6,000-estimated shaft horsepower Pratt & Whitney T34-P-6 propeller-turbine (turboprop) engines.

EMERGENCY LEAVE

BY PFC. PAT PATTON

In May, 1962, I was a heavy-duty wheel and track mechanic in the 6th Ordnance (Direct Support) Company–7th U.S. Army, at Neckarsulm, Germany, which was a Redstone missile base some 50 miles north of Stuttgart.

I knew at the time that my mother was ailing with various forms of cancer but, just 18, I didn't really realize just how bad off she was. While I was at work one day the company first sergeant approached me and said, "Pat, box up your tools and come with me." And before I knew it, I was standing in front of the company commander's desk. He said, "We're going to send you home on emergency leave. Your mother's going to have a major operation and your father wants you to be there. It doesn't look too good." I was told to pack up and be ready to leave the next morning for Rhein-Main Air Base near Frankfurt to catch a military flight back to the states.

Worried and saddened about my dear mom, I still loved airplanes, and, after the horrible nine-day trip over on the troop ship *William O. Darby*, I was more than relieved that I was going to fly this time. Better still, I boarded one of my all-time favorites—a Lockheed C-121 Constellation.

I had only flown two times before, once in a Fairchild F-27 Propjet and once in a Douglas DC-3. After I boarded the C-121, I was very surprised to see that its seats faced aftward. The reason for this was simple; that is, you'd be better protected in a crash landing (your back and not your face would be pushed forward). We were to make a stop in the Azores, an island group off the coast of Spain, to refuel, then proceed on to McGuire AFB in New Jersey.

I was seated just aft of the starboard wing and got a window seat. I recall a few things about the flight, which I'd like to share. First, since most of the flight was in the nighttime, there was a steady stream of engine exhaust fires shooting aft some three feet or so. Second, the engines were constantly moaning and groaning. And third, since the total flying time was about 18 hours, I was struck by how long the flight seemed to be. The flight seemed especially long after I boarded a 707 for the remainder of my trip to Seattle, Washington. That flight only lasted seven hours, and if I correctly remember, the distance to Seattle from New York is about the same as from Rhein-Main AB to McGuire AFB. But timewise, it was 11 hours shorter.

So I can easily understand why the demise of propliners was so sudden after the appearance of jetliners. Still, I'll always remember my association with the Connie. And looking back, for old times, I'd prefer a Connie ride over a 707 ride. And if for nothing else, outdated as it was at the time, it got me safely over the Atlantic and well on my way home to see my mother survive her operation.

The number seven L-749A built for the USAF (msn 2607) sits in plain dress and VIP transport VC-121A markings at an unknown time and location. Its final disposition is unknown. *A. I. Reveley via Dave Menard*

Both services had many subvariants of the military Super Connie. But this is beyond the scope of this reference.

NASA Connies/Super Connies

NASA, often in need of cross-country transportation by its engineers and so on, used three former USAF Connies. These included one C-121A (48-613) and two C-121Gs (54-4065 and 54-4076).

Even the U.S. Army employed a Super Connie, a lone JC-121K (ex USN WV-2, BuNo 143196) for use as a missile tracking platform. Though it carried U.S. Army markings, the mostly white airplane retained the USN Bureau Number.

Two foreign countries, India and Indonesia, procured nine and three L-1049s respectively. India got two L-1049Cs, three L-1049Es, and four L-1049Gs. Indonesia received three former Pakistan International Airlines L-1049s (one L-1049G and two L-1049Hs). The Super Connies of India were used by the Indian Navy, and the Super Connies of Indonesia were used by the Indonesian Air Force.

With engine number four running, this VC-121A is to start the other three engines for flight. Powered by four 2,500-horsepower Wright 749C-18BD-1s, the VC-121As were capable of 358 miles per hour at 19,200 feet; cruising speed was 327 miles per hour. The USAF phased out its fleet of C-121s in April 1968, after 20 years of service. *C. Cook via Dave Menard*

Following the initial flight of the first of two WV-1s (ex PO-1W) on 9 June 1949, the USN ultimately ordered 118 WV-2s (ex PO-2W) also to serve as CIC and AEW aircraft. These improved Super Constellations were redesignated as EC-121Ks in 1962 and came powered with the same engines used by USAF C/VC-121As. This plane (Bu. No. 141319) was photographed in August 1971, at a storage and disposition facility. It last served with the VW-11 (Navy Weather Squadron Eleven). *J. Sherlock via Dave Menard*

This USN WC-121N (ex WV-3; Bu. No. 137896), formerly of VW-4, is shown in storage in August 1971. Carrying a high-powered search-and-track radar system, these "navalized" Super Connies were instrumental in defining enemy aircraft during the Vietnam War. Once locked on, they guided such notable fighters as F-8 Crusaders to their targets for their kills. *J. Sherlock via Dave Menard*

USAF Air National Guard Super Connies

Beginning in 1962, as turbojet-powered transports started to become available to USAF/MATS, piston-powered cargo/transport aircraft such as the Super Connies were shifted to USAF Air National Guard (ANG) units. These are as follows: The headquarters of the ANG at Andrews AFB, Maryland, used three C-121As and one C-121C for some nine years (early 1967 to mid-1975) as transports for ANG staff members; the Mississippi ANG or MANG used as many as eight C-121Cs until April 1967; the New Jersey ANG employed nine C-121Cs and one C-121G until 1973; the ANG of Pennsylvania or PANG used 14 C-121Cs, 13 C-121Gs, and four

This May 1964 portrait of an EC-121K (Bu. No. 137889) at the Naval Air Development Center, NAS Johnsville, shows the extremely sleek lines of the Super Connie, albeit without the dolphin-like shape of earlier L-49s. *Ron Picciani via Steve Ginter*

An excellent in-flight view of a USN EC-121K (Bu. No. 141325) from VX-8 during Project Bird's Eye. Named the *Arctic Fox*, it was used for the project to improve environmental forecasting techniques used in antisubmarine warfare operations over the North Atlantic from 1962 to 1972. *Ron Picciani via Steve Ginter*

EC-121Ss until 1979; Washington, D.C., ANG used a single C-121C for 12 years (1957 to 1969); the West Virginia ANG operated C-121Cs and C-121Gs until 1972; and the Wyoming ANG or WANG flew 12 C-121Gs until 1972.

USAF Reserves Super Connies

The Air Force Reserves or AFRes was a limited user of Super Connie aircraft. Headquarters AFRes used one C-121C through the year 1972. The 79th Airborne Early Warning and Countermeasures Squadron (AEW&CS), based at Homestead AFB, Florida, employed 26 Super Connies until 1978. These include two C-121Gs, nine EC-121Ds, and 15 EC-121Ts.

The USN asked Lockheed for its proposal on a navalized version of the Starliner, to be designated W2V-1 and used for AEW duties. Lockheed came up

To obtain accurate information on the world's magnetic field, Project Magnet was begun in 1951. This USN NC-121K (Bu. No. 145925), named *Paisano Dos* (the friend) with a road runner on its nose, operated with VXN-8 (Oceanographic Development Squadron Eight). Noteworthy are the two wingtip-tanks under its fuselage, which allowed for 1,200 additional miles in range. *Ron Picciani via Steve Ginter*

While at Atsugu, Japan, this USN WC-121N (ex WV-3) was used by VW-1 while on temporary duty from its home base, NAS Barbers Point, Hawaii. VW-1 has the distinction of being the Pacific's first land-based AEW squadron and the first USN unit to receive the navalized Super Connies, beginning in 1953. *Nick Williams via Steve Ginter*

USN Blue Angels number eight (Bu. No. 131623) was a C-121J (ex R7V-1). The C-121J Super Connie variant was powered by four 3,250-horsepower Wright R-3350-91 Turbo-Compound engines and was capable of 320 miles per hour at an altitude of 20,000 feet. The Blue Angels used this plane for support operations until it was replaced by another Lockheed type, a KC-130F Hercules. *Ron Picciani via Steve Ginter*

Most color schemes on USAF aircraft before camouflage were pretty spectacular indeed. But after the advent of U.S. involvement in what became the Vietnam War, the colorful paint jobs gave way to jungle camouflage dressings. This USAF C-121S Super Connie sports the camouflage paint in late 1982, long after U.S. involvement in Vietnam. *Ron Picciani via Steve Ginter*

This USAF C-121 (msn 67-21481) was formerly a USN EC-121K (ex WV-2) redesignated EC-121R for combat operations near the demilitarized zone separating North and South Vietnam. After operations in the late 1960s and early 1970s, it was put out to pasture at the Aerospace Maintenance and Regeneration Center, Davis-Monthan AFB, Arizona, where it was photographed in February 1972. *J. Sherlock via Dave Menard*

Shown at its base in South Vietnam in August 1971, this EC-121R (msn 67-21471) had been obtained from the Navy (ex EC-121P, ex-ex WV-3). Stripped of their radomes, these Connies were used for specialized electronic missions in the Vietnam War. *J. Sherlock via Dave Menard*

with a four-turboprop- and two-turbojet-powered, radome-equipped offering, designated in-house as the CL-257 (Lockheed model 84). As offered, it was to be powered by four Allison T56-A-7 propeller-turbine engines and two Westinghouse J34 turbojet engines, mounted on either wingtip. It was to have both the radome of the WV-2 and the rotodome of the WV-2E carried jointly on its dorsal spine. The navy liked the design, and in the spring of 1957, ordered two examples. But when the 1958 budget for military expenditures was set, there wasn't enough money for the plane, and in July 1957, the program was canceled.

The USAF likewise looked at a version of it to ultimately replace its fleet of RC-121s. The Lockheed CL-344 version for the USAF, as proposed,

This C-121S, piloted by USAF Lieutenant Colonel A. Bruder, prepares to take off from its Korat, Thailand, base in September 1969. These 553rd Reconnaissance Wing aircraft were used for the most part as airborne listening posts along the infamous Ho Chi Minh Trail. *Dave Menard Collection*

never left the drawing board, for the same budgetary reasons.

In summary, for many years, the Connie and Super Connie aircraft served the U.S. armed forces very well indeed. And with its procurement orders over the years, in addition to the purchase orders of the airlines, Lockheed was able to manufacture 233 Connies, 579 Super Connies, and 44 Starliners for a grand total of 856 aircraft in all. The strikingly beautiful airplane that started its life as a prime people-mover in the form of the L-49 Constellation in the early 1940s had metamorphosed into a multifaceted aircraft for both military and civilian use, and culminated in the L-1649 Starliner of the late 1950s.

History shows these aircraft were used far longer than originally planned. Luckily for us buffs, quite a number of them are flying today.

This EC-121T (USAF sn 53-554), formerly RC-121D and EC-121D, is on public display today at the Pima Air & Space Museum. This particular Connie was first delivered to the USAF on 14 October 1955, and began operations with the 552nd Airborne Early Warning and Control Wing at the same time at McClellan AFB, California. In August 1980, after 241,095 airframe hours, it was dropped from USAF inventory as surplus. *Kirsten Oftedahl*

With one engine out, this RC-121D Super Connie (USAF sn 52-3425) lands at Otis AFB in August 1959. At that time, this airplane was used much as the Boeing E-3 Sentry or Airborne Early Warning and Control (AWACS) types are used today, but with more emphasis on reconnaissance. Of course, as with all C-121s, they doubled as troop and cargo transports. *P. Paulsen via Dave Menard*

The third of a batch of six EC-121Ds, ex RC-121D (USAF sn 53-3400), poses in-flight off the California coast. This was the last and most important version of the model L-1049 procured by the USAF. Most, if not all, of these EC-121Ds (so redesignated in 1962) saw action in Southeast Asia. *Lockheed Martin Corporation via Jeff Ethell*

LEFT: This is the first PO-1W, later WV-1 (Bu. No. 124437), on a manufacturer's flight test prior to delivery. These model L-749A Super Connies were powered by the same engines as their civilian counterparts, four 749C-18-BD1s. This was the first version to carry an additional allotment of fuel in the outer internal wing tanks, increasing its range 1,000 miles over the L-649s. *Lockheed Martin Corporation via Jeff Ethell*

CHAPTER 4

CONSTELLATION SETTING

On 26 October 1958, Pan Am inaugurated regular passenger service with its new and advanced four-engine, turbojet-powered Boeing 707 Stratoliner. With this action, the age of U.S.-designed, -built and -operated jetliner travel had begun. Soon to follow was the 880 and 990 series of jetliners from Convair (later Lockheed-Martin), and the Douglas (now Boeing) DC-8 series of jetliners. Suddenly, the dominance that had been enjoyed by the piston-powered and propeller-driven airliners was about to end. The Connies, Super Connies, and Starliners began to disappear below the horizon.

Without reservation, from the mid-1940s through the mid-1960s, the Connie was "Queen of the Skies" in civilian air travel. While it is true that Boeing's 377 and Douglas' DC-7 propliners were famed on their own merits, it was Lockheed's Connie series that was the most revered by paying passengers. And with the arrival of the jetliner, it was the end of an era.

The same held true for the U.S. armed forces. For with the arrival of the Boeing 707, starting with USAF orders for derivative C-135 Stratolifters and KC-135 Stratotankers, the demise of its C-121 fleet of aircraft was imminent. And of course the U.S. government, still in need of VIP transports, opted for the Boeing VC-137, another version of the 707, to replace its VC-121s. Slow at first, these prop-to-jet plane replacements gathered speed over time and by the mid-1970s, one would be hard-pressed to find an operational Connie at any government air base. Yet, having served the U.S. military in World War II, the Korean War, and the Vietnam War, the C-69, C-121, WV, and R7V series

Beginning service on 1 June 1957 with flights between New York and Paris, TWA Starliners began nonstop flights between Los Angeles and London and London and San Francisco on 30 September 1957. These latter flights took 19 hours and 10 minutes eastbound. *Lockheed Martin Corporation*

This overhead view of a Quantas Super Connie (H-EAM) and the first L-1649 Starliner (N1649) illustrates a lengthened fuselage, an all-new wing planform, increased vertical tail area, and for a quieter interior during flight, the more outward placement of the two inboard powerplants. The Starliner prototype made its first flight on 10 October 1956. TWA, first to order Starliners, bought 29 examples, which it called its Jetstream fleet. *Lockheed Martin Corporation*

Air France procured 14 model L-1049G Super Connie aircraft, this being the first one (F-BHBA). Shown in close-up detail is its number three and four 3,400-horsepower Wright 972TC-18DA-3 Turbo-Cyclone compound engines. First flown on 7 December 1954, the Super G was the most successful version of the Super Connie; the type first entered service with Northwest Airlines on 1 July 1955. *Lockheed Martin Corporation*

Air France Super G number one begins to taxi out for its first manufacturer's test hop in mid-1955. This version of the famed Super Connie series was capable of cruising at 305 miles per hour at 20,000 feet, with a 1,100-feet-per-minute rate of climb. In other words, to reach an altitude of 19,998 feet, it took 18.18 minutes under best conditions. *Lockheed Martin Corporation*

A Connie belonging to Aerochago S.A. of Santa Domingo, Dominican Republic, sits at Miami International, Florida, in March 1990. Through 1992, this airline was the largest operator of Connies, with one L-749, one L-1049, one R7V-1, and one C-121C; a C-121A was added later. *Steve Kinder*

An Aerochago S.A. Connie, operating out of Santa Domingo in March 1990, is just starting its engines. Aerochago used this one, their only C-121A, for transporting varied cargo. Originally USAF sn 48-614, it now crn HI-328 (2). *Steve Kinder*

of Connie aircraft are still favorites among their many devoted fans.

With the arrival of the jetliner, it was time for both domestic and foreign airlines to retire their fleets of propliners. TWA, by far the biggest user of Connie types, retired its last Connie on 6 April 1967, to end almost 22

As Lockheed's Constellation series of aircraft began to sink below the world's horizons, it marked a sad time in aviation history as this derelict Aerochago S.A. Connie shows in March 1990. *Steve Kinder*

Derelict and rotting away at Sebring, Florida, this L-1049H (N469C) was being only used for ground training exercises in early 1990. Still useful then, it helps train fireman and bomb detection personnel in an ongoing effort to make airline travel safer. *Steve Kinder*

years of continuous service, during which time over 50 million passengers rode these truly magnificent airliners.

TWA's radar-equipped Super Gs featured the industry's first "dual-class" configurations, according to Mike Machat. Included in TWA's dual-class arrangement he added, "There was a luxurious lounge, complete with rich wood paneling and a hand-painted

THE CONNIE AND ME

BY JANE BOMAR MILLER

Trans World Airlines hired me in 1944. Our training class was the first one that didn't require that potential flight attendants must first have a degree in nursing. After our six weeks of stewardess training, we were domiciled in various U.S. cities—myself in Kansas City, Missouri, TWA's corporate headquarters. My flying routes usually consisted of flights from Kansas City to New York, and vice versa. Also from Kansas City to either Los Angeles or San Francisco, and vice versa. These flights on the average lasted about four hours.

The arrival of the Connie was quite an event at TWA, a beginning of a new age—pressurized flight. Since they could fly at much higher altitudes than earlier TWA airliners, there was far less turbulence and a large reduction in airsick passengers.

Two hostesses were assigned to every flight, plus three crew members in the cockpit—pilot, copilot, and flight engineer. Most of the passengers in those days were on a high-priority ticket, because seats were hard to obtain. On our passenger list could be an Arabian prince or two, a planeload of Hollywood movie stars on War Bond drives, or even John F. Kennedy on his way to San Francisco to attend the first-ever gathering of the United World Congress (now United Nations).

I had served on Douglas DC-3s and Boeing B-307s earlier, but in my eyes, the Connie was by far the best propliner I had ever flown on.

Being in the right place at the right time, as they say, does have its rewards. For on 15 November 1945, I was fortunate enough to be on the first delivery flight of a Connie to TWA. It was piloted by Bob Buck, copiloted by Jim Combs, flight-engineered by John Collings, and my hostess partner was Pat Bigson.

I married TWA Captain John Miller in 1947, and because married women were not allowed to serve as stewardesses, my flying career was quickly grounded. But all in all, I loved my job. Especially when I met the Connie and one of its pilots.

artist's mural, plus eight sleeping berths for first-class passengers (who occupied the quieter aft fuselage section), and identical pressurized comfort for those seated in the forward coach cabin." He concluded, "Although faster than earlier model Connies, the Super G's flying times still allowed gracious and elaborate food and bar service for Ambassador First Class passengers; meals were available for purchase in Golden Banner Coach."

Other major U.S. airlines such as Capital, Eastern, Flying Tigers, National, and Northwest followed suit and retired their Connie/Super Connie fleets.

The major foreign airlines like Air France, KLM, Lufthansa, QANTAS, VARIG, and Trans-Canada operated their fleets a bit longer but, in the jet age, likewise retired them.

The three initial users of the L-1649A Starliners—TWA, Air France, and Lufthansa—started retiring them in the early 1960s. Three Starliners reportedly were being used in 1976 as airborne cattle cars by Burns Aviation.

This ANSA (Aerolineas Mundo S.A.) C-121C (HI-515) was in operation out of Santa Domingo in March 1990. This airline also operated an L-1049H, which it got out of storage at Sanford, Florida. *Steve Kinder*

A close-up of an EC-121Ts search-and-track radar system components shows, if nothing else, that even with these monstrous appendages, a Super Connie was still good looking! One appendage was the Identification Friend or Foe/Selective Identification Feature shown forward of its dorsal radome. *Steve Ginter*

This very clean EC-121T (53-535) was on display with a Boeing B-47 Stratojet, Douglas C-124 Globemaster II, and other notable aircraft at Pima Air & Space Museum in August 1976. These aircraft participated in many important projects during the Vietnam War. This EC was assigned to the 551st AEWCW Wing, and was based at Otis AFB, Massachusetts. *Steve Ginter*

For 16 years (1942–1958), Lockheed produced its Connie, Super Connie, and Starliner series of aircraft. No less than 856 of these being built and delivered, the first one in April 1943, and the last one in February 1958.

Loved by military personnel attached to them, USAF Crew 28 of operation College Eye during the Vietnam War came up with the *Ode to a Connie*: "Listen to her rumble, she rattles and she roars, she flies over many countries and off of many shores. She'll fly for sixteen hours and climb to nineteen-five, and she will still be flying—in nineteen eighty-five."

Revered as "easy to fly and naturally graceful" by an EC-121D crewman Donal Born, he said, "Above all else—she was 'Always a Lady.'"

Born's feelings are, this writer thinks, pretty much how the rest of us Connie lovers feel. Although many of them have been scrapped or left to sit derelict somewhere awaiting their final fate, many have survived to be enjoyed by museum goers or by those lucky enough to see the fully restored and still flying examples. If not for organizations such as the Connie Group, Save-A-Connie, and the Confederate Air Force, those of us who haven't seen a Connie fly would never be witness to their airborne poetry in motion.

This is one of four L-49s purchased by Air France in the late 1940s. Out to pasture near Paris in March 1974, its final disposition remains unclear. Originally owned by Air France, it appears to be permanently parked, and this writer does not recognize its markings. *Steve Kinder*

The most recognizable feature of the Connie is its tri-tailed configuration. This and the dolphin-like profile (more prominent on the original Connies) set them apart from other types of aircraft. The badge is of the now decommissioned Aerospace Defense Command or ADC of the USAF. *Steve Ginter*

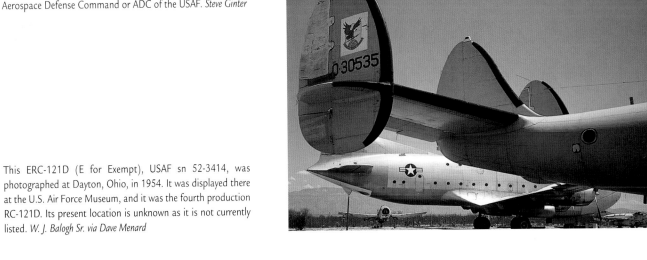

This ERC-121D (E for Exempt), USAF sn 52-3414, was photographed at Dayton, Ohio, in 1954. It was displayed there at the U.S. Air Force Museum, and it was the fourth production RC-121D. Its present location is unknown as it is not currently listed. *W. J. Balogh Sr. via Dave Menard*

ROUTE OF THE STARS
BY ANITA DEVARNEY WHITE

I was employed by TWA at LaGuardia Airport, New York City, from December 1942 to 30 August 1946. When first employed, we flew U.S. routes only. TWA was famed for its East Coast/West Coast service, called the "Route of the Stars," mainly because of the Connie's great range. Howard Hughes, part-owner of TWA, and his Hollywood motion picture group earned us that name.

I saw many famous names on passenger lists and met some of them—and even photographed Ingrid Bergman. My job, in the Flight Control Dispatch Center, was most exciting! I handled flight logs, provided weather reports, and recorded the radio check points. What I'm getting to here is the excitement we felt when the Connies were finally handed back to us in late 1945, after their use in the war.

As you know, in the years before World War II, Howard Hughes and Jack Frye had specified with Lockheed their requirements for a super kind of an airliner—one to hold more passengers, fly higher, fly farther, and cross the U.S. non-stop. Just as this fantastic airliner started to be available to us, the U.S. Army Air Forces ATC grabbed them up.

Finally at the end of the war, the Connies—those built for TWA and used by the military—were returned to us. It was a happy and interesting time for us.

Meanwhile, TWA management was hard at work establishing overseas routes. Some of these first routes involved Paris, Madrid, and Rome. Then, due to this, Transcontinental and Western Airlines became Trans World Airlines.

In early 1944, rumors began to fly about a "press" flight—planned for publicity. Finally we got a tentative date for the publicity flight—17 April 1944. We listened for a teletype message to confirm this. And on the morning of the 17th, we heard of TWA Connie number one departing the West Coast. Six hours, 57 minutes, and 51 seconds after takeoff, it landed at Washington, D.C., in record time. And before returning the plane to the U.S. Army, they flew up to LaGuardia.

Numerous VIPs were onboard and some of them came up to operations. Among them was Danny Kaye, whom I met. In no time, they were all over our offices—Howard Hughes and Jack Frye too! Since they were crew members, they had to report to dispatch. As part of dispatch, it was a most thrilling time for me.

They were in New York City for a good part of the following week. There were parties and public appearances with the many celebrities and TWA management. Mr. Hughes shot landings with the Connie—all day once at the airport. I remember we had to get him three different crews, for he exhausted the legal time of the first and second crews to complete his day!

Crew scheduling was also done out of the operations office. On his last day in New York, because of his extra long day of flying *his* new bird, he slept in the crew lounge at LaGuardia. He left a wake-up call—my job—and I remember being somewhat apprehensive about his temperament. He had a bad reputation of being arrogant, demanding, stern, and gruff. When time for his wake-up call, as I approached the crew lounge door, he called out: "Up!" before I could even knock on the door. Whew! What a relief! Only then did I realize just how scared I'd been to wake him up.

All in all, it was a great time for me—a part of aviation history, and I'm glad I was there. What's more, I remember how much better the Connie was over anything else I'd been previously associated with. Recently, in June 1996, I saw an advertisement in *Newsweek* Magazine celebrating 50 years of transatlantic service, 1946-1996. It made me proud to have been there, more than 50 years ago, when it all started for TWA—thanks to the Connie.

This was the 26th RC-121D (to EC-121D in 1962) produced for the USAF (sn 53-533) as it appeared in September 1982 at Otis AFB, Massachusetts. Carrying Semi-Automatic Ground Environment (SAGE) electronics, these aircraft, in part, directed ADC fighter-interceptors to their target aircraft. *Ron Picciani via Steve Ginter*

NEXT: Stored at Camarillo, California, in March 1996, this C-121C (N73544), formerly USAF sn 54-156, is nearly restored. It had most recently served with the ANG Bureau as a personnel transportation airplane. *Steve Kinder*

This former Aeronautical Systems Division C-121C (54-160) has been put out to pasture at Davis-Monthan AFB. During its active service it was used as a VIP transport. The photo was taken in August 1971. *J. Sherlock via Dave Menard*

In April 1972, this C-121C (54-181) was captured at Andrews AFB about 11 miles southeast of Washington, DC. This 'C' was at that time used by the ANG Bureau. It's shown in military inspection shape; compare it to the ANG Bureau C-121C at Camarillo Airport. *Steve Miller via Dave Menard*

A combat veteran of the Vietnam War, this EC-121R (67-21497) parks in front of a Boeing KC-97G at Davis-Monthan AFB. This Super Connie began life as a USN EC-121K (ex WV-2) and, as an EC-121R, it was used as an airborne relay platform to receive Air-Delivered Seismic Intrusion Device (ADSID) signals, which detected troop movements behind enemy lines. *B. R. Baker via Dave Menard*

Arguably the best looking of all military Connies was the Blue Angels' C-121J (Bu. No. 131623). It is a tribute that one of the world's best-known aerial demonstration teams chose a Connie to transport its support personnel. One can only imagine a Connie in the colors and markings of the world's other best-known demonstration team—the USAF Thunderbirds. *Dave Ostrowski via Dave Menard*

APPENDIX

Major differences between the Constellation, Super Constellation, and Starliner types (original versions)

	Constellation	Super Constellation	Starliner
Wingspan	123 feet	123 feet	150 feet
Length	95 feet, 3 inches	97 feet, 4 inches	116 feet, 2 inches (radar nose)
Height	23 feet, 8 inches	22 feet, 5 inches	23 feet, 4.8 inches
Gross weight	86,250 pounds	107,000 pounds	156,000 pounds
Cruise speed	313 mph	330 mph	342 mph
Maximum speed	339 mph	355 mph	376 mph
Payload (maximum)	18,423 pounds	20,276 pounds	24,355 pounds
Range (maximum)	2,290 miles	2,600 miles	5,410 miles
Ceiling	25,300 feet	24,100 feet	23,700 feet

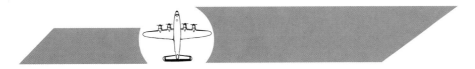

BIBLIOGRAPHY

Articles

Bowers, Peter M. Constellation. *Wings*. Sentry Books, Inc., October 1990; Pt. 1.

Bowers, Peter M. Constellation. *Airpower*. Sentry Books, Inc., November 1990; Pt. 2.

Books

Francillon, Rene J. *Lockheed Aircraft Since 1913*. Putnam and Naval Institute Press, 1982, 1989.

Ginter, Steve. *Lockheed C-121 Constellation*. Naval Fighters, 1983.

Goldberg, Alfred (Editor). *A History of the United States Air Force, 1907–1957*. D. Van Nostrand Company, Inc., 1957.

Knaack, Marcelle Size. *Post-World War II Bombers*. U.S. Government Printing Office, 1988.

Stringfellow, Curtis K., and Bowers, Peter M. Lockheed. *Constellation*. Motorbooks International, 1992, 1993.

Documents

Johnson, Clarence L. *Development of the Lockheed Constellation*. Lockheed Aircraft Corporation, November 1944.

INDEX